Growing Up Mental: A Son's Story
Karriem K. Kanston

This book is not intended as a substitute for the medical advice of physicians. The reader should consult a physician in matters relating to his or her health and particularly with respect to any symptoms that may require diagnosis or medical attention.

Copyright © 2022 by Karriem Kanston

All rights reserved. No part of this book may be reproduced or used in any manner without written permission of the author except for the use of quotations in a book review.

For more information, address:
kkanston@kanston.com.

ISBN 978-1-7350328-7-0

www.tfieldinglowecompany.com

TABLE OF CONTENTS

Introduction: Mother Angela Kanston

Chapter 1.
The Beginning---Page 1

Chapter 2.
Discouraged to be Encouraged------------------------------Page 22

Chapter 3.
Many Roads One Path to Choose---------------------------Page 32

Chapter 4.
Perseverance---Page 42

Chapter 5.
Power of Encouragement-------------------------------------Page 62

Chapter 6.
Defining and Operating in Your Purpose------------------Page 72

Chapter 7.
It's Not About How You Start But How You Finish---Page 78

Appendix A: Resources

Appendix B: Facts About Mental Health

Appendix C: Tips and Suggestions

Appendix D: GLOSSARY

Appendix E: Works Cited

Introduction
≈
Mother Angela Kanston

My mental illness started after the first year of my marriage when my husband and I started having marriage issues. My husband also had mental and drug problems. I could not handle it.

I left and went back to my parents after my first son was born. That's when I had to be hospitalized for three months. I never had that type of trauma in my life before, ever. My oldest son was traumatized as a baby and then throughout his life. That's why he wants to stay a big child and have fun because he was traumatized even in my womb when I was carrying him.

When he was a baby at five months old, I took him, and I was running down the street at night with him wrapped in a blanket in the dark down a block in Brooklyn in the middle of the road because I was so paranoid. I thought everyone was trying to take him away from me. My mother began to run after me, yelling, "Angie, we are just trying to get you help. " We both could have got hit by those swerving cars. My father came behind my mother. Somehow, she was able to get me into the station wagon and bring me to Kings County G building Psychiatric Building. That was the beginning of my mental illness journey. This never happened to me until I married my first husband, and our marriage had so much trauma.

I often felt so helpless and knew that all three of my sons felt feeble and hurt when my family brought them to the Kings County G Building. I repeatedly yelled out of the screened windows to my three sons and cried. And my three sons would shout back, "Mommy, when are you getting out of there? What's going to happen to us and who will we stay with?" I thought that was enough to make my heart come out of my chest.

I did not know how I could stop the hurt feelings that the three of my sons felt. I asked God, "Is this happening to me and all of us also?" But you know we cannot choose our battles or the situations and deadly blows that life gives us. I had to pray that we would get through every second because it felt like it would never end. I got to hope when I saw male family members step in and be like a dad or big brother to my three sons. Thank God the three of my sons have good souls and know that the Lord, who is everything, is with them. That's why they made it through it all. Not your mother, not your father, not anybody can take the place of God's love and deliverance.

Karriem's Parent's Wedding Day

Grandpa Cody on Left
Harry Kanston, III & Angela Cody

CHAPTER 1: THE BEGINNING

When you think about the beginning of something, you usually think about a start date. Putting a start date on when I first recognized my family wasn't typical, was impossible. I genuinely do not know exactly how young I was when I figured out that my parents grappled with mental illness. Still, it didn't take long for me to realize that something was different with my family. Even when the concepts of mental health and mental illness are too big for young children to grasp, it's easy for them to recognize when things aren't normal in their house. They can compare to how family and friends live and see that their parents aren't typical. I grew up knowing my family wasn't typical, but that doesn't mean I didn't love them or aren't grateful for the life they gave me. This story is simply about me. In writing this book I wanted to turn the spotlight on mental illness and share what families, especially children, go through while dealing with loved ones who struggle with mental illness. More people need to be educated about the emotional and physical strain mental health has on families. My mother wrote the introduction of this book to give you a window view into the world of someone who struggles with mental illness. My mother is a person who overcame many challenges during her life's journey. My father, who also struggled with mental illness, is no longer living. It would have been nice to get his story from his perspective, but we can only go by my memories. Throughout this book, I try to express that their journeys are not my journey, and their stories are not my story. Yet, as my parents, their stories have directly impacted my stories. They have influenced the man I became today. Without the parents I had, I would not be the person I am, and I am grateful. I respect them, their trials, and their triumphs.

Many will say - why would you write a book like this? Why would you discuss the intimate or private things that have happened in your life? Weren't you told that what is said in this house stays in this house? Airing our dirty laundry is not done in the Black community. In my life, I have already heard many statements like this, and I have risked many relationships. Some family and friends have stopped talking to me because I have shared my experiences of growing up. I know I am striking a nerve with people, but I want to share truths and propel others towards action. Faith without works is dead. We must use our faith, which is hoping during the unseen, to embrace the seen.

Black and Brown communities in the United States, and even more so around the world, historically struggle with talking about mental illness. Our people feel there is some stigma attached to psychological openness and seeking help in general, which makes them hesitant to talk about mental health.

Young Karriem

The National Alliance on Mental Illness states that Black people are about 13% of the population but account for 16% of people suffering from mental illness in America. This disproportionate statistic can be pointed back to slavery. This is especially true for those descendants of people who come from the lineage of African slaves in America. I could not even imagine what my ancestors went through, first, by being enslaved by another African in Africa, then being put on a slave ship and traveling to the Americas, surviving the journey only then to be sold as property to White people, free labor, generation after generation. According to Professor Michael J. Halloran (2019), after slavery, people thought they were free, but the psychological trauma continued and was passed down as intergenerational cultural trauma which continues today. In other words, the anguish caused by slavery resulted in poor mental health. These sufferers who became parents passed down their struggles to their children and so on through the generations, resulting in a high number of African Americans struggling with mental health today. The trauma that was felt became ingrained in the culture, it became part of life, passed down through generations. In addition to cultural trauma, Black people in America have faced racism, higher rates of poverty, higher rates of incarceration, and unequal access to education, all of which add to mental health disorders.

Knowing this, we must encourage and support the Black community to speak openly about their struggles and end the silence. One of my goals in writing this book is to help my community feel empowered to speak out about their struggles with mental health. We must normalize discussions around mental health. If we don't talk about it, we cannot solve the problem. When we open up, we can encourage others to do so, and so on until the stigma is removed. There are many organizations currently trying to fight the stigma of mental health in the Black community, including The Boris Henson Foundation, The Steve Fund, and The Black Emotional and Mental Health Collective. They are opening up the lines of communication and offering resources to our marginalized communities. For more information see Appendix A.

During the time I spent writing this book I had been reading and watching the story of Prince Harry and Meghan Markle as they struggled with being part of the royal family. They both had roles to play in a family where silence was key. Similarly in the Black community, we do not let people know what is happening in our families and that is part of our culture. Seeing Prince Harry and his wife break their silence and share their story encouraged me to share mine. I know many people feel more comfortable suffering in silence. We hesitate to tell our story because we think that it will

show we are weak or incapable of triumph. We don't want to ask for help, especially with something that might make us look different or strange. What we often don't realize is that when we are silent, we deny ourselves the help we need. We are not only perpetuating the stigma of mental health, but we are denying ourselves healing. If we don't speak out and express that we are in need, how can we expect to ever heal?

To use an analogy, when people are trapped in the rubble of a collapsed building, the rescue workers sometimes ask everyone to be silent. This is because the rescuers might hear a noise like someone screaming for help or someone banging on a pipe to get attention. The person who is trapped and calling for help is expressing that they cannot get out of this situation alone. They need to be rescued and are trying to say "hey, I'm here, come help me." Many people who struggle with mental illness in their lives are trapped and cannot get out because they are silent. They are afraid to call for help because they think their friends, family, or society will label them in some way. Others might think we are weak, overly dramatic, or worse, maybe they won't believe us when we ask for help. I want you to know that caring people and professionals in this world want to help. They want to come to your aid and assist you on this journey.

Our culture needs to be liberated from the trend of being silent about mental illness and being silent about the physical and emotional effects it has on families. We have allowed too many people to remain silent, lost in their fears and tears. By sharing a piece of my life, I hope I can encourage open conversations among families. I want to encourage other people to feel comfortable with the facts of their stories. Trust me, when you share your story, others might not like it. However, it is your story, and only you can tell it from your side. You lived it, and you experienced it the way you experienced it. Even if others were around, they did not know the context of your personal story. It is your right to tell it in your voice, to have your struggles known, and to ask for the help you need. The goal is to heal instead of keeping on covering the infected wounds.

I remember as a young child talking about other people at family or social gatherings. There would be some great mystery surrounding certain people. As a child, I wanted to know what was going on – why my uncle, auntie, or cousin wasn't having fun at the party with everyone, or why some of them didn't come at all. I would be told, "that is just how they are." This confused me even more - what do you mean that is just how they are? I couldn't figure it out. Reflecting on this as an adult, I now know that it is just what we, as a community, were conditioned to say about people who struggled with mental illness. These people in my family were hiding their struggles instead of reaching out to their family for help. As I said before, even as a young child, I could sense that something was wrong with that being the norm. It seemed strange that we would brush something like that under the rug instead of supporting our family as we did in all other situations. When someone was ill physically, we would all rally and support them – why wouldn't we do the same for mental illness?

For a long time, society has dismissed people who struggle with mental illness, and, for many years, they did not receive treatment. Throughout history, God knows how many of these people were locked up in institutions or put away from the public. There was a time in America and around the world when people endured treatments such as shock therapy and scores of drugs. Sometimes the supposed cure for mental illness led to more pain and even death. In the late 1800s and early 1900s, America built many asylums for people who struggled with mental illness. It was how society and the government thought best to deal with people who were struggling with their mental health: put them all in one place, out of the way. Society did not truly understand these people or their struggles, thus they were not worthy of integrating into society. It's no wonder that communities grew to fear sharing their struggles with mental illness when help, for a long time, meant isolation or dangerous and painful treatments. The humanity of these people was taken away and they were considered less than because of something they couldn't help – because of a disease. This calls to mind what Africans went through when they were turned into slaves and brought to America. Someone determined one life was worth less than another life, that someone had the right to lock up another person and treat them as less than a human being. Can you imagine? Your humanity is taken away, and now you are considered less of a human being because someone decided it was so. In the end, the Lord frees all those who are wrongfully imprisoned – whether by man or by their minds.

Galatians 5:1 ESV

"We have been set free; stand firm therefore, and do not submit again to a yoke of slavery. "

Mental illness is a struggle, which can be very discouraging for family and friends who have a loved one suffering from this disease. Part of my purpose for writing this book is to let others know that there are people who care and professionals who can help. This book was written not only for the people who struggle with mental illness but also for the family and friends helping someone with this difficult and often life-long journey. In writing this book, I wanted to turn the spotlight on mental illness and share the struggles of families, especially children living with loved ones who suffer from mental illness. The experiences of those who are affected by mental illness, not just the sufferers but also the important people in their lives, are valuable stories. These stories can become an inspiration for others who are facing the same struggles. I hope that when people hear my story, they will feel less alone and want to find out how to break themselves out of the silence.

"Mental illness can be like you are on an emotional roller coaster, and you are trying even out the ups and downs you are experiencing. " – Thea Fielding-Lowe

You Break, or You Persevere

I was born in Queens, N.Y., on February 26, 1976, to Harry Kanston III and Angela (Cody) Kanston at Miriam Immaculate Hospital. The hospital was closed in 2009 due to a lack of funding. My mother recalls that I didn't want to come into the world easily. I resisted and tried to stay in my cozy space for as long as possible. While my mother and father were the people used to bring me into the world, I did not choose them. I had no choice in the matter. As we all know, you do not have a choice in who your biological mother and father are going to be. We must make the best with the lot we are given. I'm not upset about who I was born to or how I was born. It's just a fact that these were the parents given to me, and I had no choice but to make the best of it. I am thankful that God used these two people to bring me into the world. I thank my mother for carrying me for nine months. I thank God for the love that my parents had for me and my siblings. While there were many struggles, we also had great times, and my mother continuously does important things for my brothers and me. Throughout my story, I want to stress that my parents showed us love, and my brothers and I always knew that we were born out of love. I am the youngest of three boys. My oldest brother's name is Hassan, and my middle brother's name is Akbar. As you can guess, our names are Muslim because my parents were practitioners of Islam when we were born. I have not followed in that path and have since become a follower of Jesus Christ, serving the Father, Son, and Holy Spirit.

My mother and father both dealt with mental illnesses such as depression, bipolar disorder, and schizophrenia. I cannot imagine all the struggles and challenges they faced in their lives while living with these illnesses. I could only consider how it affected my brothers and me. Over the years, I have talked with many people who suffer from mental illness, and they typically will say that a person cannot imagine how they feel or what they think unless you have the same illness. As a person who grew up close to those suffering, I think this is very true. It is hard to be empathetic when someone is struggling with something you have never experienced and something that can often be completely invisible. It's easy to simply say – just get over it, or just don't think that way. However, that dismissive attitude is more hurtful than helpful, and we must recognize that even if we can't relate, our loved ones are suffering from something that is very real, very painful, and often very frightening. When we can show empathy, it can make it easier for our family and friends to open up about what they're experiencing. Letting them know that we care about their struggles allows them to share their experiences more freely and seek help with less fear of being further marginalized. Part of our jobs as loved ones for those who struggle is to not only be a listening ear but to at least try to understand where they are coming from.

Again, I don't know what age I was when I realized my parents suffered from mental illness. What I did notice at an early age was the disorganization in my family. We moved countless times, sometimes living with different family members because our parents couldn't provide a stable home for themselves, never mind their children. It was so hard to see them struggle with their issues and to have those issues so deeply impact our family. My father, for many years, struggled with addictions such as drugs and alcohol, in addition to mental illness. While I don't have experience dealing with these vices personally, I saw firsthand how my father struggled. Living with addiction and mental illness was no joke. When you battle addictions and mental illness simultaneously, they compound on top of each other. Additionally, according to Mental Health America, when you have co-occurring disorders like mental health struggles and addiction, your chances of recovery are far less, and your chances of a health crisis are far higher. Many people turn to addictive behaviors to escape the pain and fear of mental health struggles, making it even more critical to get professional help for a loved one early.

One night that lives in my memory clearly shows the struggles that people with co-occurring disorders have. My father had come home after battling his demons and was so lost in his mind that he thought the living room was the bathroom. I remember screaming at him and saying, "Dad, there is no toilet here, and this is not a bathroom!" I do not think it registered, but he continued to pee in the living room. As a son, it was very difficult for me to see my father in that state of mind. I respected and still respect my father despite all his faults, even though he is not living on this earth. For men, as sons, we typically look to our fathers to show us how to be a man. My father did that in some instances but also failed in many other areas. Seeing a man struggle with providing for his family is a tricky thing. As a son, you feel hurt because your father couldn't give a stable life for his family continuously. I cannot even imagine what my mother went through as a wife and mom with a husband who struggled with such vices.

My father was born in the South but, when he was young, moved with his family to New York City. My father's life included the Civil Rights movement, the Vietnam war, the rise of crack and cocaine, and the policies and laws of calling Black men and Black boys super predators. I cannot imagine what my father and his brothers endured growing up in a society in which one's manhood was devalued and questioned by those in power. To be stereotyped and feared when you, as a person, had done nothing to deserve this other than being born in a particular culture and born a particular color. As I mentioned, I no longer have my father to interview for his story, but we can assume that these events that impacted so many had a huge influence on his life.

My father was an entrepreneur and a hard worker. He always wanted to provide for his family, and he did have years of being stable at various times in my childhood and my young adult life. One thing I vividly remember is that when he couldn't provide for his family, he would get upset. What caused him to be upset, I'm not completely sure, but I have a strong sense that his idea of manhood was that he had to provide for his family. I do believe that a man should provide for his family if he has the means, knowledge, and wisdom, but this is not the only and number one priority of a man. In my mind, the priorities of a man should be, in this order, God, self-care, your spouse, your children, and then your work.

You must first have a relationship with God. He is the one who created you and allows you to do His purpose on Earth. In times when you feel you are alone, God will be the friend you can turn to. He is always by your side, and having a strong relationship with Him, I have found, will benefit all areas of your life. God's power can lift you in your darkest times, and having Him by you during the celebratory times in your life gives you an even deeper appreciation for the good. Just as without my parents, I wouldn't be the man I am today; without God, I would not be who I am.

Next, self-care is critical. You cannot help anyone else until you help yourself. Being healthy – mind, body, and soul – is especially important for a well-lived life, but even more so when we are responsible for the care of others. We cannot give what we do not have within us. Self-care looks different to many people. This can be seeking mental health help for yourself, making sure your physical health is taken care of, or finding an outlet for stress and frustration. Having a hobby, spending time with friends, or taking time with things you enjoy are also great ideas for some 'you' time. Additionally, whatever spirituality you follow, it is important to take time in your day to practice. My Faith and relationship with God are particularly important to my self-care when it comes to my spirit and soul. Everyone has a limit on how much stress they can handle. When the limit is reached, we boil over very quickly, becoming frustrated and in a space where we cannot handle it anymore. By prioritizing self-care, we can ensure that our stress level is regularly decreased and set back to baseline. Many people brush this off as not important, especially when we are busy caring for family and balancing careers, but you are no use to anyone else if you cannot manage your own mental and physical health.

Having a strong relationship with your spouse or significant other is so important when times get hard. Building a bond where both of you celebrate what you bring to the table will strengthen each other. Think of it as filling in the gaps you have. No one is perfect, we all have shortcomings, but your spouse or significant other can help bridge those gaps, and together, through your partnership, you are stronger. Also, having a spouse or significant other allows for another viewpoint on your life. If you open up and allow them to know you intimately, they can provide you with advice and support. They can allow you to be vulnerable in a way that you cannot be with anyone else. Don't take them for granted.

Once couples begin to have children, they tend to put

their offspring in a place of priority before their spouse. However, your children should come after your spouse. For you to have the strength and patience to raise children, you must be in one accord with your spouse. I know this might sound controversial as children need so much from us and are generally thought to be every parent's priority. While, as parents, we do have the responsibility of taking care of them, nurturing them, and helping them grow so they can successfully conduct their purpose on Earth, we cannot do that if there is tension in the home. You and your spouse must build a united front, two as one, on every avenue of your life together – even children. As I said before, you both bring unique gifts to the table. You can find balance in that and be secure, so your parenting will be unified. Having a companion in your spouse, someone you can rely on, allows you to have a place to vent frustrations as a parent, someone who can help you through the tough times and make strong decisions – together.

Finally, as a man, it is important to be able to provide for your family. I take pride in my career and business. This isn't to say that your spouse can't also help, but providing for your family is both a great responsibility and a great joy. Unfortunately, as I mentioned, my father wasn't always able to accomplish this priority. There were many times when one of the five priorities would fall apart, and rather than continue fighting or fixing the issue, he would flee. As a son looking from the outside, I think my father wanted to be able to have all five of these priorities working right in his life. He would have these great spurts of being stable and taking care of his family. Unfortunately, his mental health being what it was, things would turn out of control, and as soon as one priority fell apart, he would leave instead of fight. Dr. Samuel Chand, a great speaker, and author, authored a book titled *Leadership Pain.* In his book, he talks about how a leader will never go past their highest pain level. What I gathered from this idea is that every person, including my father, has a threshold for pain. The pain that he experienced from not being able to fulfill his priorities met his threshold quickly, and he was unable to manage that.

Occasionally my father had interactions with law enforcement, but I thank God that he did not lose his life when he had episodes requiring help. Over the last year and a half, we have been getting a full view of the stories of Black males who might have struggled with mental illness and were mistreated by or killed by police. It is horrific that someone should lose their life when they are going through a mental health crisis. When the police departments do not have adequate resources and the right first response team to handle these issues effectively, the worst outcome is often the case. This is another reason why there must be a greater awareness of the struggle of mental illness for Black males. We are taught to be the providers, strong for our families but are forgotten when we have struggles and need resources. If the head of a household is removed, then there is a potential that the entire house will fall. While there are organizations such as NAMI, Boris Henson Foundation, Black Emotional, and Mental Health Cooperative, and others that are helping the Black community with mental health, there needs to be more individuals talking about their struggles to normalize the stigma. See Appendix A for a more extensive list of resources.

I hope to help normalize the stigma by sharing the stories of my life living with family members who struggled with their mental health. One of the most impactful stories in my life that, I feel, made me versus breaking me was the beginning of my college journey. As a young man, I could not focus on going to college right after high school. I think the reason was that most of my teachers talked about the labor trades. Also, I just wanted to graduate high school and make some money. Going into the armed forces would be my route to a good salary with benefits and a free college education during my service. It all sounded great, my path laid out for me, but God had different things in mind.

I signed up for the Army National Guards in my junior year. At the same time, I also started attending the Upward Bound Program at Queens College. The Upward Bound Program geared you to go to college after high school. It was one of the catalysts to get me to apply to colleges. I ended up applying to Johnson & Wales University in Rhode Island and, after getting accepted, chose to attend. My parents generously agreed to help me pay for college so that I would not have to take out many student loans. I set off to Rhode Island, excited to begin a new adventure. Unfortunately, the day before I was supposed to start, I received a call from my parents stating that they could not pay the tuition. That call rocked my world. I felt like my life was about to spiral downward. I was discouraged and understandably upset. I remember tasting pepper in my mouth and choking a little. Then I heard God's voice saying, "I brought you this far, and I have given you a plan to prosper. Karriem, you will not fail. Keep moving forward. You are here at this college for a reason, and keep moving forward." He told me to forgive my parents, reminding me, "If you harbor hate for them, you will never succeed and break free from generational curses that plague your family."

Listening to God's word, I decided to stay in college. I developed a plan and strategies to complete my education. I had to persevere beyond what the facts were telling me, that I was statistically likely to end up with struggles like my parents. I had to persevere beyond what I was seeing unfold in front of me. I had to move forward and act on faith. Of course, not everything went smoothly, but the rocky start gave me the determination to push through and graduate with three business degrees. This situation taught me that when we are face struggles or trials in our lives, they can break or make us. It is not easy to persevere during hard times. We must make that conscious choice to keep moving forward.

Jeremiah 29:11 NIV
"For I know the plans I have for you, declares the Lord. Plans to prosper you and not to harm you, plans to give you hope and a future."

Some questions you can ask yourself after reading this chapter:

1. How have your cultural or familial expectations around mental health impacted your view?

2. How have the mental health stories of those in your family affected you? Think about all areas of your life; emotional, financial, time, plans, and relationships.

CHAPTER 2: DISCOURAGED TO BE ENCOURAGED

I'd like to begin this chapter with a question to help focus the discussion: *how do we go from discouragement to being encouraged, especially when there is suffering from a mental illness and trauma?*

Think of a time when you felt discouraged. What caused your discouragement? It could be your life, your career, or your family. Discouragement comes when we do not have hope. I have spoken to many adults who are living with discouragement because of how their parents or legal guardians raised them. They point out that they are discouraged because their past was so harsh that it inhibits their future. Discouragement holds us back. Additionally, many family members with loved ones who struggle with mental health may feel discouraged, as if they are giving constantly and seeing no benefits. Part of this goes back to the self-care we discussed in the previous chapter – being able to increase our capacity – but also learning to celebrate the small steps rather than focusing on the life-long struggle.

When I was growing up, I often felt trapped by my parents' lifestyle. Their choices deeply affected my brothers and me both on a physical day-to-day basis but also emotionally. Living with inconsistency and stress,

I never felt like my life was settled. The fact is that I moved fourteen different times from birth to eighteen years old. This is true, not just made up just to sell books. Just imagine a child being moved from place to place, never any stability or consistency in their home. They start to get to know people, and then they have to move, meet new friends, go to a new school, develop new routines, learn the surroundings of their recent living quarters, etc. When this continuous instability happens to children, they feel they are in a whirlwind. Children are wired to look for stability, and when that is uprooted, they can become discouraged.

I was very disheartened as a young child and especially as a teenager. I felt like my parents didn't care about me because I didn't live with them for the entirety of my childhood. I feel that every child has a natural or spiritual connection to their parents. No matter how messed up the parents may be, there is still a connection to those used to bring you into the world. As children, we do not understand things the way that adults do. As children, our brains are still forming and learning. We're still building our mental filing cabinets and becoming the people we were meant to be. As children, we recognize that adults are meant to be our protectors and that they have the power to make decisions for us. When adults only provide instability and fail to protect the children in their care, that's when the child becomes discouraged. Children know that adults are responsible to care for them, and when it consistently doesn't happen, they lose hope. Just imagine you are used to driving to a particular destination for many months and years. One day you get halfway to where you are going, and now there is a long detour. Many people would get frustrated and flustered by taking another route. Some of us would get anxious because we are not used to something new. Children experience this when their lives are uprooted and changed. When it happens over and over, they learn they cannot rely on the adults in their lives, they lose hope. They also might act out in unusual ways because they are not feeling safe.

Safety is one of Maslow's essential hierarchy of needs for a human being. In a 1943 paper titled "A Theory of Human Motivation," American psychologist Abraham Maslow theorized that our decision-making as humans is influenced by a series of five basic needs. These needs must be met for humans to be able to fully function in a mentally and physically healthy state. They include psychological, safety, love and belonging, esteem, and self-actualization. When one of these needs is not met, chaos ensues. The child acts out, chooses bad behavior, can become oppositional, and can develop mental health issues as an adult.

I am not saying I experienced trauma constantly in my youth, but now that I reflect on it probably felt that way for me as a child, particularly when I didn't know where I would live, who I would stay with, and what school I would attend when my parents were struggling. My needs for safety as well as love and belonging were not being met. This led me to seek it out from relatives and family or friends. I thank the Lord that the places I lived in when my parents couldn't provide a roof over my head were stable and brought normalcy to me. I thank those caregivers that chose to take me in as a kid and provide for me and my brothers. They allowed me to see what normalcy looks like in a family.

I feel that when you are raised in such a way, you either mimic that way, or you learn from it and do better. As an adult, I recognize how important it is for children to feel safe – physically and psychologically – and loved in a home where they belong. My needs not being met as a young person helped me to recognize, as a parent and grown adult, what my children need. I can make sure that all of their needs are being met because I know what it feels like to not have them met. I am lucky that the path for me was to learn from my parents' mistakes and not repeat them.

Studies show that children who grow up in unstable homes are more likely to face trauma in their family structure, with lasting effects as they grow. An article published in the Indian Journal of Psychology Medicine (2017) stated that a "disruption in family structure could lead to several adverse events impacting children's mental health." I can remember so vividly the training that my wife and I took through the Department of Children Youth and Families when we were going through the process to be foster parents and how they trained us to understand children who faced trauma in their lives. They taught us to understand specific traumas and explained that kids who have experienced trauma and raised in unsafe environments will act out or do bizarre things. When anyone is put into an uncomfortable situation, not just adults, they are not just acting out. Their bodies, soul, and spirit are put into safety mode. Safety mode is for when you are in surroundings that you are not used to or surroundings that feel unsafe - when things are not familiar. This looks differently for many people, and for some, especially children, it looks like acting out or bizarre behaviors. Remember, children do not have the capacity to rationalize their feelings and only know to express their trauma and hurt in primitive ways.

Kids do adapt to their new environments very quickly. Educators say kids are like sponges. They soak up everything that is in their environment. We know that whether kids are in a good or toxic environment, they will reveal the signs from the environment they grew up in. What you see and experience in your environment shall come out of you. We, as adults, can look at our past trauma and try to deal with it more rationally and productively. When we're trying to heal our minds and bodies, we begin peeling back the layers of our past and realize that much of our struggles as adults stem from what we went through as children. I think about that, especially with my older brother. As he is older, he was with my parents and dealt with the chaos longer than my middle brother and me. Today he still struggles with life and the past hindering him as an adult.

All the trauma children face causes discouragement at an early age through adulthood. Forgiveness is the first step to overcoming discouragement and moving on to being encouraged. At the age of eighteen, I decided to forgive my parents for how I was raised. I had to let go of the hurt and pain I was holding on inside of me. It might seem that writing this book proves I have not forgiven them, but that isn't the case. Even though I have forgiven them, I clearly have not forgotten, and I'm not suggesting we should forget. Forgiving and forgetting are not the same things. When we forgive others, we are allowing ourselves to move on from the pain they have caused us. We are releasing ourselves from holding on to the dark hurt in our hearts. However, we can still remember what happened to us and learn from it. I understand that many of the things that happened were out of my parent's control, and they tried to do the best with what they were given. The Lord asks us to forgive others so we can be forgiven. The Lord is about love, and I strongly feel we should love others as He loved us.

Matthew 6:14
"For if ye forgive men their trespasses, your heavenly Father will also forgive you. "

Before we can even begin to forgive any wrong done to us in the past, we must fully understand the whys of what happened. Within families, the only way to do this is through open and honest communication. This can be exceedingly difficult as often people don't want to admit to things they think will have negative consequences, will hurt themselves or others. It is really necessary to begin healing, however. My family, on both my mother's and father's sides, have struggled with mental illness for generations. I learned about the history of our family once I became an adult, but I feel that open communication and honesty could have helped me much sooner. If I had been allowed to learn about the mental health my family struggled with at an early age, I could have been more understanding about the life we were living. It could have brought us closer as a family and given me a reason for what was happening to us. Telling me could have assisted me with understanding what my parents have been through. This also could have prepared me as an adult to deal with my parents' struggles. We must have open communication in families, particularly those dealing with illnesses like mental health, that will impact everyone.

Now that I know my family's history, I am encouraged! Knowledge has helped me understand my parents' struggles and allowed me to strive to break the generational curse of mental illness. I can look for signs of mental illness in myself and tell my doctors accurate information about my family medical history to be preventative. Suppose you go to your primary care doctor for the first time and during your continuous care. In that case, they always ask you questions about your parents' and grandparents' health history. They are trying to determine if what you are experiencing now as a symptom or an illness is hereditary. So, the things you are facing as struggles can be traced back to your family history. Knowing your family's past is not only important for being able to navigate life with them but also for your own health.

Open communication is critical for another reason. We must be allowed to develop empathy for our loved ones going through mental illness. If we're left in the dark with no understanding of their struggles, it prevents us from truly recognizing their pain. Part of the judgmental nature of society comes from ignorance. We don't take the time to listen to people's stories before they have a chance share. We just shut them down because of selfishness and sometimes fear. So many people with mental illness feel unheard and isolated with no one to be there for them. When there is no hope, no help in sight, there is no vision of a better future. It is easy to feel discouraged when you feel that you have no outlet, no escape from your own mental prison. As family members of those with mental illness, we must strive to be a shoulder to lean on, someone who is willing to listen and strive to understand. We should be supporting individuals who struggle with mental illness and encouraging them to grow in their purpose. When we encourage, discouragement decreases. Allow yourself to become a champion of people. Someone is waiting on you to encourage them to break out of their trials and tribulations.

It takes courage. An interesting thing about the word "discourage" - it is made up of the word "courage." We must be courageous, no matter what side of this struggle you are on. It takes courage to talk about your mental health struggles, to open up, and let others know they are not alone in this. It takes courage to be a caregiver and give yourself over to service for the sake of a friend or family member. It can be a lot of responsibility to care for someone suffering from mental illness, but it's worth it. We are put on this Earth to help one another, to help each other be the best versions of themselves that they can be. When we encourage others through either sharing our stories or providing them with support, we are doing the works of God.

Some questions you can ask yourself after reading this chapter:

1. What in your life has left you feeling discouraged? Recognizing the problem is one of the first steps in overcoming it.

2. How can you encourage open communication within your family?

CHAPTER 3: MANY ROADS, ONE PATH TO CHOOSE - SAVED BY GOD'S GRACE

Honestly, no one can tell you how you should feel or what you should do with the life you have been given. They can provide you with insight, but the only one that can give you clear direction is the one who created you. He knows your purpose and destiny. The number one person I count on daily is God. My truth is that I know that without him, I could not have gotten through what I went through and continue to face as a Black man in America. When I think about the struggles we went through as a family, I realize it's not so much what we went through but how I got through that truly matters. By the Grace of God, through his everlasting love and protection, I became the man I am today.

The story of finding my faith begins when I was in junior high. Throughout my childhood, my parents would often separate. They would eventually come back together after some time apart. However, after one separation, my mother did marry another man, while we were living in Yonkers, NY. Our stepfather, Yasin, had a good-paying job and provided stability. Thinking back, he reminds me of myself now, as a mild-mannered man. Children like stability, and he showed us what we had been missing for years. We lived comfortably with him for a while until my father came back onto the scene. He caused a rift between Yasin and my mother, eventually breaking them apart, and then my parents got back together.

Initially, when my mother and Yasin separated, we were staying at my grandparent's house in Flatbush, Brooklyn, New York, where I attended Lefferts Junior High School. I remember helping my Aunt Tenzy after school, selling Avon products to people on Nostrand Ave when they came out of the train station. I liked that a lot; helping my aunt, who also helped me. My Aunt Tenzy, and the rest of my mother's family, tried to show me as much love and stability as they could. I have some strong memories of Tenzy, like drinking coffee with her and when she would put me on the ice chest at my grandma's house. I was the youngest grandchild on my mother's side, so I was protected and kept out of trouble. I believe this was one of the times in my life that God stepped in to shelter me from harm and dangers. See, even if you don't know Him, He still knows you. God protects children who can't protect themselves. Now don't get me wrong, there have been horrible things that have happened to children. God didn't do these bad things, but he allowed the enemy to mess with us on Earth. The enemy is trying to get us off our road to our eternal destinies. He uses devices such as our temples to get us off the infinite destiny road that God has for us. Shortly after junior high, I found my place among God's righteous, preparing myself for eternal life.

After my mother and father got back together, we moved to Elm Street, Yonkers, New York. Things went well for a while. During that time, I went to Islamic School Sister Clara Muhammed Private School in Harlem, NY. It was a strict school, but it had a good curriculum. My older brothers Hassan and Akbar also went to my school, and we traveled together. Each way we took a bus then a train as the school wasn't near our house. However, before too long, my parents found themselves without a place to stay.

After New York, then we were off to Virginia. We soon stayed with my aunt - my father's sister - and her two children. I remember the house was very small and packed with eight people. Also, at my aunt's house, I was introduced to the smell of chitterlings, a southern delicacy, being cooked in a skillet pan. They smelled so bad that I didn't even want to be in the same house as them. To this day, I have never eaten them because of that memory, despite how many people find them delicious.

When my parents finally got enough money to get our own house, we moved and rented a house on 27th Street in Newport News, VA. It was a large yellow house with a lot of room and a large yard to play in. As a kid, it was great that we had a 7-Eleven and McDonald's, every kid's playground, nearby. What I loved most about Virginia was the people's friendliness and the fact that it wasn't a huge, busy city with tons of people. The South had quite a different atmosphere than the Northeast, and I fell in love with living there.

While living on 27th Street, I became friends with a great family by the name of the Parkers. They lived two doors down from me in Newport News. They had two sons about my age and an older daughter. Their house became, for me, a safe place. Like my stepfather and my mother's family in NY, the Parkers' house was stable and loving. As a child, I was drawn to that environment like a dying man in the desert is drawn to water. I needed the balance in my life that this family had in abundance. Remember, children need stability and need to have an environment that is predictable and shows them, love. Children need stability as they are growing in their youthful life on Earth. When children have a setting to thrive, they will. When their environment is in disorder, it is hard to truly see a child's potential.

The Parkers would invite me to their home, and whenever I would go, they would always offer me something to eat. I suppose it was a taste of southern hospitality. The parents both worked and spent time with their kids. One day they invited me to go to church, and I said yes. The Parkers would go to church a minimum of three times a week and believed in the Father, Son, and Holy Spirit. Even though I was raised

Muslim, I never felt that I was a Muslim. I decided to go to the church with this family because I felt something was pulling me. Church with the Parkers became another safe space for me. The Church was a Pentecostal Church with Bishop E. Carr as pastor. His entire family was involved with the ministry; his children would sing and play instruments. They also had another church in North Carolina. I remember so much about this church, but the most vivid of memories is the love all the people had for each other. Praise dancing and speaking in tongues were the norm during services. When the Holy Spirit was moving, the organist would hit a key, and then everyone in the place would shout, scream, holler, and praise dance. Man, this was an incredible sight! To this day, I love to see this form of praise.

Going to church and spending time with the Parkers opened doors for me that would have otherwise remained closed. For example, there was a point when I was singing in three different choirs. We also formed a singing group with the Parkers and another friend. We would travel around to churches and sing songs by the Winans Family. While I wasn't the best solo singer, I did well with the group – it was good for my confidence and my spirit. Now being brought up in an Islamic household was quite different from the church I was going to with the Parkers. I had been to a Christian church with my other family members and was always around Christian folks. This time it was different. I remember one night when I was fourteen, I finally decided to surrender my life to Jesus Christ. I knew right away that it was the right decision. I had not found God; God had found me. I confessed the Sinner's Prayer and did my Roman's Road to salvation. I was free from sin and now walking on the path of righteousness for an eternal heaven.

God did not tell me I would no longer have trials and tribulations. Soon after that, my parents' mental illness reared its head again, mostly with my father. My father was a different man when things were going well for him, and when they did not go right, everyone was affected by his struggles. My mother and father lost the house we were renting on 27th street and had to move to a shelter. It was then that Akbar, my middle brother, and I decided that we should move back to New York City to live with our family there. Hassan, the oldest, decided to stay with our parents.

In the summer of 1991, my brother and I moved with my Aunt Laverne and her children in Bedstuy, Brooklyn, NY. I also found a job during the summer working with my cousin Lise in Upper Manhattan. I would work for a property management company refinishing wood. This was an awesome summer hanging with family and with my cousins and their mother in a cool Brooklyn neighborhood. At the end of the summer, we decided to travel back to Virginia and stay with my parents. We thought at that time they had stable housing, but they didn't. So we decided to travel back to New York.

Akbar and I moved to Queens with my aunt, uncle, and cousin. I will forever be grateful for their generosity and love in opening their house to us once again. They had a small two-bedroom home and sacrificed space, time, and money to help us. I can never repay them for what they did to provide us with that stability. Family is essential, but not just biological family. The people who are your village, neighborhood – your tribe - can provide for you not only worldly support but emotional and spiritual support as well. When people have empathy, they are genuine in who they are.

One of the most painful discoveries as a child is the loss of faith in your parents. As I mentioned before, children are born with hope in their parents – they naturally turn to their parents and caregivers for love and support. When you begin life, you have faith in your parents, you think that things will get better and that they always have your best interest in mind. However, when things don't always change or improve. This can be so frustrating and upsetting. As a child, you want your parents, your guardian, the person taking care of you to be the best version of themselves that they can be. Sometimes they can't do what you think they should be doing. As kids, we hold grudges against our parents based on bad experiences. However, because I knew – and still know- the Lord, I knew that I had to put more faith in God than my parents. If your parents can't take care of you, indeed, we have to put faith in the One who created us. The Lord that made us is ultimately responsible for taking care of us.

One of the things I've learned is that God will never fail you. People will fail us, and persevering through that can be challenging at any age. As we grow older, we have the capacity to understand that there will be dark times but that there is a light at the end of the tunnel. We can keep moving forward, focused on the understanding that our destiny is ahead of us. Sometimes we must walk towards our destiny for it to manifest, leaving behind grudges and past hurts.

I was once told by a psychologist that we as people often live in the past and not in the present or future. We hold ourselves back from a new life because we live in what we went through. We're unable to recognize breakthroughs that would help us live in a better space because we are so consumed with what we went through. It lives in our minds, we replay events and situations, wondering how we would be different if our past had been different. I have experience with this, and I understand how hard it is to move on from the past. However, that is why we need help – from friends, professionals, or just other people sharing their journeys. Whatever it takes, we must get free from the past that is holding us back. Whatever we decide, whatever path we choose, it's ours to live with. If we decide to live in the past, that is our choice, no one else's. We cannot blame what happened to us. We cannot blame others for our choice to dwell on what hurts us. As I said, moving on from the past and taking a different road can be so unbelievably difficult, but the choice is there. You just need to decide that's the right choice for you.

God has given every human being the free will to choose their path. This means we can choose to live in the past or choose to move on to a brighter life. This means that we have authority over our choices, which is as great a gift as when he gave us dominion over the Earth. God presents us with many roads that we may choose paths that can lead to a variety of destinations. I liken this to taking a road trip. We can choose a variety of routes to take, some of them will take us where we are meant to go, and some will lead to dangerous areas or down paths that lead to a dead-end. When we get to a dangerous area or even a dead-end, we might need help getting back on the road that was meant for us. This reminds me of the time I used to drive large tractor-trailers in the Army National Guard, and when we would back up, we would need an aide to guide us so we didn't crash into something. When you get to a dead end or have a challenging time getting off a bad path, it is important to find someone to help you through the process. Reaching a dead end doesn't mean it's time to give up on yourself or your dreams. It just means you need help to get back where you belong. It's a signal that it's time to reach out and get some help; reach out to your teachers, your family members, your friends, or even professionals. As I've mentioned before, asking for help can be a difficult step. We must let down our pride and admit that we have lost our way, but there is no shame at all in doing so. Even the strongest among us need help sometimes.

Some questions you can ask yourself after reading this chapter:

1. How can faith support you through times of struggle?

2. Who are the people you can turn to for support – who are the people that make up your tribe?

CHAPTER 4. PERSEVERANCE

Moving past the trials in your past can open an exciting new chapter in your life. It thrills me to think that people can use this book to help them do just that. I feel I have been called to help others find their breakthroughs, and hopefully, this whole book, but especially this chapter, can put you on the road to yours.

There is a great motivational speaker by the name of Christine Caine. Her message about "moving past your past" provides powerful advice about how to overcome significant obstacles in your life that seem insurmountable. When I listen to her speak and read her books, they are uplifting to me and help me continue to make sure that I persevere no matter what trials come my way.

Seeking resources like Christine has helped me to develop my path for overcoming obstacles. I call them the Four Principles of Building Your Perseverance.

1. **Acknowledge the problem**
2. **Decide what are you going to do**
3. **Get help, professional help**
4. **Activating your perseverance**

Through these principles, we can develop the capacity to overcome our past and move on to a brighter future.

Acknowledging The Problem

As I talk about the first principle, acknowledging the problem, I want to begin with the story of my college journey. I have mentioned some of the struggles I had when beginning college, but I feel the whole story is important to help readers understand how I began to break away from my parent's cycle of trauma. As I mentioned before, my family moved to Virginia when I was just ending middle school. Before too long, my brother Akbar and I returned to New York City, leaving our parents and older brother in Virginia. We lived with my mother's family, and I attended Andrew Jackson high school, named after our 7th President of the United States. Today, the school is called Campus Magnet school. A few famous people attended my high school, including L.L. Cool J, 50 cent, and Ed Lover. While learning did happen at this school, every day, I was reminded of the violence and issues happening just outside the doors. We were subjected to metal detectors daily, and the police were there regularly. Sometimes, it would take us an hour to just get into the school because of how many people were being checked by the metal detector. One of the most chaotic places in the school was the lunchroom. I hated that area of the school because of the chaos, so I usually never went to lunch. After living in chaos and lacking stability in my life, I preferred peace and quiet when I could find it. Part of that, too, could have been my introverted, turtlelike personality.

Despite these issues, I liked my school in my junior and senior years because I was in the Co-op program. Co-op programs allow high school students to still attend school while working part-time. I would go to academic school for one week, and then the next week, I will go to work in construction on a farm. My brother was in the same program, and we were able to work together at the same construction site in our junior year. In our senior year, my brother and I worked with Con Edison, the electrical company in New York. Through this program, I learned responsibility and how to be committed when you have a job. Also, I was around people who showed me what I needed to do to be a good worker.

The co-op program taught me to be a hard worker and that I could earn a good salary by being in the trades. This was an exciting opportunity to make money and change the trajectory of my life, or so I thought at the time. My primary goal was to get a good job after high school. I was focused on improving my finances as I had grown up poor in material things but rich in love. However, my cousin, who was in college herself, suggested I think about the college route and check out a program called Upward Bound. Upward Bound is an organization that gears high students towards college. Participating in the program allows you to take college classes while you are in high school, which was nice because before that opportunity, I wasn't even thinking about college.

The classes I took through Upward Bound were rigorous academic classes on a college campus. We would also take field trips to other college campuses; they provided help with applying for scholarships and walked us through the process of applying to colleges. It was a game-changer in my life because it made me see college as a possibility where I had always been pushed towards the trades. There is nothing wrong with the blue-collar trades, they are vital jobs in society, but I hadn't even known college could be an option for me. Through Upward Bound, I was introduced to a whole new world of opportunities.

I started my college journey in September 1994 by going to Johnson & Wales University in Providence, Rhode Island, to study business management and entrepreneurship. The college was about three hours away from New York City. Originally, I wanted to go farther south, to Hampton University in Hampton, Virginia, because of my time living in Newport News. I learned to love the south, the warmth, and the hospitableness of the people there. Unfortunately, I wasn't accepted to Hampton. I had applied to Johnson & Wales because my cousin did, and I had heard it had an excellent business school. The funny thing was, I received my acceptance letter before my cousin did, and he had applied before me! Also, I never had time to visit the campus as I was completing my Army occupational training for the Army National Guard the summer after my senior year. For me, one of the draws was that they had a four-day school week as most of the students worked over the weekend. In the end, I'm glad I chose JWU as I enjoyed my time there, and it helped pave the way for my future in more ways than one.

The day my aunt and uncle drove me up to Providence, Rhode Island, I really was excited. I was starting a new chapter and moving on in my life. However, the past continued to haunt me. As I mentioned previously, my parents had agreed to help me pay for college, but the day before classes were supposed to start, my mother called me and said she could no longer help financially. It was a devastating blow. I had such hate in my heart against my parents for being let down once again. After talking to my mother, I called my brother and had a conversation with him about what I should do. What a huge obstacle I had to face: the decision to stay in school or leave was on my shoulders.

My brother felt I should return to New York, but the decision was mine to make and mine alone. After the initial shock wore off, I didn't want to give up. I had just gotten to college, and now I might have to leave through no fault of my own! My determination won out, and I was able to stay at Johnson & Wales through a combination of student loans and working to pay my tuition. At that moment, when I learned my parents would not help pay for my education, I had two paths before me – an easy path that would allow me to give up and head home and a path that was arguably more difficult but would allow me to accomplish my goals. I chose the more difficult path. At that moment, I chose to acknowledge that going back to New York would be furthering my problems. I had to figure a way to climb out of the hole my parents had dug for us through the years. I had to recognize that relying on them was no longer serving my greater destiny and that I would have to make a go of it myself. I had to acknowledge that the problem was the emotional and physical roadblocks they created, and the only way forward was to make a life for myself. Choosing to make my path and move beyond what was expected of me will forever be a formative moment for me. I acknowledged that living in my parent's shadow, allowing them to continue having their hands in these key areas of my life was giving them power. They still had the power to traumatize me, to derail me, to wreak havoc in my life. I realized that only I could stop that, and by choosing to forge a path without them, away from my family, I did. Eventually, I earned an associates in entrepreneurship and a bachelor's in business management.

Someone is reading this book that is saying, "I'm having a tough time. I don't know what's happening. I need some help. My family is struggling. My friend is struggling. I am struggling. I do not know what to do." First, please acknowledge the pain and struggle. Be truthful with yourself about the causes of your struggle – where they are coming from and why they are affecting you. Look at your life around you and think, am I causing these problems myself? Is there someone in my life that is no longer serving me? Do I need to forge a new relationship with a friend or a family member, one where I can protect myself while still being in their lives? Once you acknowledge the problem, only then you can begin to create a plan and find the help you need from God and professionals.

In this first step, ask yourself,

1. What are the emotional and physical roadblocks that are holding you back right now?

2. What haven't you accomplished because you said you couldn't do it?

Karriem in the Army

Decide What You Are Going to Do

I decided to stay in college and find a way to pay for it. College was a place where I truly became a mature adult. I strongly felt I had to make this education thing work. In my freshmen year, I worked security as a work-study and continued my work in the National Guard. I had a blast as a freshman. I made lots of friends, was a good student, and honestly made a few terrible choices. For the first time, I felt like I was my own person. During that year, I talked with God often. I would ask why He gave me parents who struggled with mental illness. He told me those were the people He chose for me to make my entry into the Earth and that I must respect and honor them. He also reminded me that He took care of me through the mess, stress, moving, trials, and tribulations of my childhood. I had to accept God's word, not question it, and move forward on my path towards my destiny.

Over time I knew the important thing for me to do was to release the hate for my parents that was built up inside of me. Coming to this conclusion was much easier than doing it. However, once I was able to forgive, a large weight was lifted off my heart, life, and mind. I realized that the people I needed to forgive weren't dwelling on the issue like I was. Their hearts were not burdened with the past like mine was. They were moving on, living their lives, and following their own paths. I was the one that was mired down by their struggles and mistakes. God called on me to forgive so I could be free of this burden. I had the power to relieve myself of the hate that was poisoning me, and you do too. As I mentioned before, people hesitate to forgive because they think it means forgetting. Absolution is not about forgetting. Forgiveness is not about letting the people who have wronged you get away with what they did. Honestly, forgiveness is not for them. It is for you. It's about getting the weight that you are holding in your heart, life, and mind off of you. Remember, when you forgive someone, you are no longer allowing them to continue hurting you. You are permitting yourself to heal. When I did this, my purpose and destiny became more apparent, and now I could move forward to my future. Once you are ready, you will find that forgiveness will open space in your heart that was taken by hate, and you will feel some relief from the burden of your past.

Another decision I made in college was to break out of my introverted shell to build my leadership skills. My personality, by design, is that of an introvert. I love being alone, lost in my thoughts about the future. The Myers-Briggs Type Indicator (MBTI) is a fun way of discovering more about your personality based on psychological types theorized by Carl Jung. The assessment has you rate your preferences for a variety of situations and the results place you into one of sixteen categories. According to the assessment, my dominant personality style is Introverted Sensing Thinking and Judging (ISTJ), also known as a Peacemaker. This tells me that I was made to keep the peace and help others. Like Myers-Briggs, the Clifton Strengths assessment developed by the Gallup Organization helps corporations find the strengths of their workers to "improve culture and performance." My Clifton Strengths styles are Futuristic and Activator, telling me my strengths lie in planning for the future and encouraging others. This makes sense to me when I think of the situations and careers I gravitated toward in my life. Being an introverted person who thinks about the future, has skills to sense what other people are feeling, and can help others develop their goals allows me to be successful in helping small business owners and entrepreneurs in my career. However, as I said before, I could find my career path, I knew I needed to develop my leadership skills.

In my sophomore year in college, I became a Resident Assistant (RA). As an RA, I had the responsibility to take care of my fellow students and help them integrate into the college. This was a big responsibility. I was living and working in a dorm on campus, coupled with going to the same school with the people I was trying to help, presented both opportunities and challenges. In my RA position, I couldn't run from people and hide. I was the person others were running to for help. This broke me out of my shell and pushed me into developing my extrovert and leadership skills. As Dr. John C Maxwell says, people can learn to be leaders by impacting other people. I learned how to be a leader through both experiences, like my time as an RA, and also through instruction. During my sophomore year, my school started a leadership concentration which some good friends, including my now wife, and I were the first students to participate in.

Another opportunity to improve my leadership skills through experience was when I was asked to teach and train middle school children at the Times Square Academy on leadership during my college days. A professor of mine, Donna Thomsen, had recommended a few other students and me for this program. I remember feeling that this was way above my abilities and that I didn't have the knowledge or experience to teach leadership skills to youths. However, Professor Thomsen knew I had exactly what I needed to succeed in this project. During this time, I was also being mentored by John Yena, the Johnson & Wales University Chancellor. Chancellor Yena decided to invest his time and money in me by hiring a professional communication consultant named Barbara Tannenbaum. This was a huge lesson for me related to respecting professional help and understanding that it is vital to seek professional help when you have reached the limits of your ability. Although this situation was career-focused, this applies to any situation in life. When you are at your limits, get help, no matter the area of your life you are struggling in. Getting help with my communication to become more effective opened up more opportunities to help other people. After finishing college and obtaining my three degrees - an A.S. in Entrepreneurship, B.S. in Business Management, and M.A. in Teaching Business Education – from Johnson & Wales, I decided to stay and work for the University. I had the privilege of being the Director of the Multicultural Center on campus as well as teaching leadership studies and human resource classes. Seeking help is critical when you reach your capacity or limit in any sense.

Throughout my time at JWU, I was blessed to be taught by great professors. My college experiences, the people I met, and the adults who led me, showed me that once you put your mind to something, you can achieve it through determination and persistence, no matter your background or color. Once you decide what you're going to do, you have the power to make it a reality.

In this next step, ask yourself,

1. What can you do to better your situation in the now?

2. What do you want for your future?

**JWU Graduation, May 2000
Get Help, Professional Help**

I think if my father and family had more resources around us, it would have assisted with him staying in the fight. During the times when he struggled with his addictions and mental illness, he could have used support from health professionals. Also, my family probably could have used help with housing and other supports throughout my childhood. I know now that there are mental health organizations and so many more resources now where those who struggle with mental health issues and their families are provided resources.

I do not know what could have been different if my parents had received professional help when they first struggled with mental illness. Things could have turned out differently, but we can only imagine as they didn't take that path. Being a foster and adoptive parent, I have learned the importance of seeking help when it is needed. Ecclesiastes 4:9 says, "Two are better than one because they have a good reward for their toil." When you turn to someone else for help, it benefits you in multiple ways. First, you are sharing some of your burdens. The other person can help carry your load for you. Also, the person you're turning to may be more knowledgeable than you are when it comes to managing mental health issues or whatever it is that you are seeking help for. I can remember when I didn't have any more answers or ideas to assist my mother during a time of struggle with her mental state. She brought me to meet with her social worker, who gave me some encouraging advice. The social worker told me that when I was at my total capacity with helping my mother, I needed to turn the help over to mental health professionals. This was some of the best advice I have received that continues to pay dividends. Why go it alone when you can get help?

One thing to keep in mind is that no one fully knows

your journey but you and God. Yes, we can get the needed professional help, but we must go to the One who created us for proper support as we go through our life's journey. When we turn to God with our problems, we also unburdening them, and He can speak to us in our hearts and provide us with answers no one else can.

In Appendix A, I have included a list of recommended professional resources. This list is not exhaustive, you can find reliable resources in your area. Consider talking to your primary care doctor for recommendations if you are looking for mental health support or any other type of health care resources.

In this third step ask yourself,

1. Now that you have decided what you want to do, how can you improve your life and move forward towards your destiny, who can help you achieve this?

2. What professional resources do you need to help you move forward?

Activating Your Perseverance

I talk about perseverance a little bit in Chapter 1, but I want to elaborate more on how to build perseverance. My first tip is do not be afraid to fail. That seems to be contradictory that failing is ok when we're talking about moving forward. However, when we fail, we can take the opportunity to learn from the failure. When things get tough, we want to move past the strenuous part of our lives quickly, but sometimes when we are in the valley moments, we are being conditioned to be stronger.

Many people have asked me, "how do you sustain yourself and continue to persevere despite everything your family has gone through?" My number one response is that God has given me patience and the gift of perseverance. This is not to say that perseverance has come easy to me. It is still a tough road, especially when there is a large mountain to move out of the way. We are all human beings, we all have ups and downs in life, but the trick is learning how to push through the downs to enjoy the ups to the fullest. When we are down low in valleys, we do not see or know the answer to why we are in the dark place currently in our lives. When we get out of that difficult place, we understand something clearly at last and can reflect on why God put us through this trial. We can ask ourselves what went wrong, how can we avoid it in the future, and what the whole situation taught us about ourselves. Every experience in life – whether we perceive it as a failure or a success – can teach us a lot about who we are. As much as personality tests are fun and informative, our reactions to everyday life can say just as much about us. Think of a time when you experienced a failure and consider what your response was during that time of failure. There is so much we can learn about what makes us tick and how we can improve and grow. Failure teaches us to be resilient, to never give up, and to keep pushing forward. Without failure, we wouldn't have a reason to do, win, or get over something. We must believe that we are strong enough to make it through. We must also remember that God has us experience everything for a reason, and we are never truly without Him.

Psalm 23:4
"Even though I walk through the valley of the shadow of death, I will fear no evil, for you are with me, your rod and your staff they comfort me. "

My next tip for building perseverance is to lean on the One who created you. When I depend on God when things get tough, it lightens the load I must carry. I understand that not everyone knows the Lord as I do, but if you have God in your life, He is a major resource for you to tap into. If you don't have God, at the very least, find a friend or family member who can help push you forward. As I mentioned in the previous step, having support – whether it's from God or another person – makes the journey more surmountable. When you get into a challenging situation it is easier to persevere with help. Don't go to war just by yourself, someone should have your back.

My final tip for perseverance is that you must make a conscious choice that you are going to persevere. Before you even hit a roadblock you must come to terms with the knowledge that it will happen, that you will struggle and stumble on your journey. Once you recognize that, you can make the vow to yourself that you will keep going no matter what. In dark times your senses are probably going to tell you to give up. Your friends and family might tell you to give up as my brother did when I was facing my choice between college and returning home. If you have already chosen to keep going, if you already made that decision, it will be easier to persevere when you're facing something that seems insurmountable. That choice won't be something you debate over – you will already know the answer and have more of a drive to not give up on yourself. You had already decided what you want to do, and it will be time to just do it. You will move forward toward your destiny. When we move forward, it's not always in leaps and bounds. Perseverance doesn't guarantee that things will be easy, and you will just breeze right through times of struggle. You must take one step forward, one inch, one second at a time. The important thing to remember is that you are doing it, you are making it through, and if you can hang on in these increments, it will be worth it. This process might be slow, but you can achieve greatness. I hope to encourage my readers to keep pushing on through trials. Every breath that you are given each day allows you to walk in your purpose.

Some other questions you can ask yourself after reading this chapter,

1. How do you react in times of failure, and what does that tell you about yourself?

2. Who do you call on when you get into a challenging situation?

3. Who is going to encourage you to get out of that challenging situation?

CHAPTER 5: THE POWER OF ENCOURAGEMENT

One factor that will aid in persevering through your dark times is finding encouragement. In Chapter 2, Discouraged to be Encouraged, we talked about turning your discouragement into encouragement. We all, as people, will face challenging times during our life. As I mention in Chapter 4, it is important to have others in our life that we can rely on and turn to when we need help. However, aside from God, one of our most important resources is our own self. When we can encourage ourselves, we are also building the capacity to help others and become their helping posts. Through encouragement, we can lift ourselves and others.

One of my greatest sources of encouragement is my wife, Deborah. While I was at Johnson & Wales University, one of my jobs was through work-study as a security guard. I basically had a post in a residence hall where I would watch the main hall, supervise who came into the building, and would report any serious issues to the security officers. One day while I was standing at the front door, I saw a beautiful, tall, dark, lovely woman walk out of the building with her friends. As soon as I saw her, my spirit began to rise. God was telling me there was something incredible about this woman. The next time I saw her was in a literature class that we both happened to be taking. I learned her name was Deborah. Having class together was a fantastic opportunity for me to try to build a relationship with her since we would see each other at least twice a week. I desperately wanted to get to know her, but I was afraid to approach her. I asked a friend to introduce me, but that didn't work out, so our freshman year passed, and I never got up the courage to ask her out. However, God and fate had something special in store for us.

In my sophomore year, I began my leadership studies concentration, including taking several leadership classes. In the first leadership class I walked into, Deborah was sitting there. I sat right next to her because I told myself I would not allow this opportunity to pass again. Despite being in the same class again, I still did not dare to ask her out. One day we were both attending a gathering at another local college, Brown University. After the gathering, I saw Deborah going to her friend's car. I ran to her and said, "here's my number. Give me a call." I felt that if she called, then this relationship was ordained by God. The next day, lo and behold, she called. We had a lengthy conversation, and I guess you can say that started our deep relationship.

We married on December 31st of, 2000. I asked my wife's mother if I could marry her, and she said yes, so we began the planning. We were married in New Jersey during a snowstorm. We thought things would get shut down, but we had faith and moved forward with our ceremony. My mother and father did attend the wedding, but my family being how they are, we always had to search for them at certain critical moments during the event. One of the wonderful things about my wife is that she is the only child in her immediate family and meshes so well with my family. Our wedding cemented this by us bringing both families together, and everyone had a great time. To this day, our families always talk about the lovely day. One of the best days of my life was when I married my wife with the blessing of God. Proverbs 18:22 says, "he that finds a good wife finds a good thing," and I thank the Lord for the wife that I found in Deborah.

One thing I love about my wife is that she is a person who can be around anybody and always be helpful. She helps me to stay motivated and encourages me through my life, career, and entrepreneurship. By nature, she is a very steady and detailed person.

I thank God that no matter what problems or issues I have faced with my family's mental illness, she has always been supportive and able to steady me. For instance, when we bought our first house and began renovating to make it a home, my mother and father began struggling again. My father moved to Las Vegas with his parents, and my mother was stuck in Virginia by herself. I decided to invite my mother to move with us. Before I made that decision, I did not talk with my

Wedding Picture

wife. I had made the decision in my mind, but I knew that it wouldn't be right for our family unless Deborah agreed. She did, and I thanked her for making the tough decision. We knew that having my mother live with us wasn't going to be a bed of roses, and we were right. Moving my mother into my home wasn't easy and did put some strain on my marriage. While we knew there would be some road bumps, I hadn't really thought through the situation well enough. I was young and thought I had all the answers. I had talked to my wife previously about my parents' struggles, but I still hadn't revealed all of the struggles my mother faced. This goes back to open and honest communication with your family. Also, we didn't take the time to think through the type of bumps we might face and plan how we would overcome them. Had we thought about the difficulties of living with a person with mental illness, we might have developed a list of resources and made some preemptive decisions that could have helped in the long run. Unfortunately, we weren't so forward-thinking, so when those problems arose, we were stuck trying to figure them out on the fly.

After a while, my mother didn't like the way we lived and was not shy in telling us so. Having two women in the house butting heads and me the male, produced issues. This was increased by the fact that my wife and I were still building our relationship as a married couple. This was also made worse by the fact that all my experience in dealing with my parent's mental illness happened when I was a child – I didn't have experience living with my mother as a twenty-something adult. This handicapped me and often brought me to the limits of my capacity.

The power of encouragement came to me during this time in the form of my wife, Deborah. As an outsider to the mother-son relationship, she could see things that I couldn't see. She could see when I reached my limit when helping my mother and reach out to me. She encouraged me to say, "I reached my capacity. I need help." I tended to try to go it alone in a lot of things, but two minds are better than one.

Now, encouragement can be internal or external. For me, sometimes it was external, like in the form of my wife, and sometimes it came from within me. The power of encouragement can also come from places that we do not even expect. I can remember one day I was asking for help when going through a tough time. A person who didn't even know me and struggled with their mental and addiction issues encouraged me that everything would be alright. Their kindness and empathy helped me get through that moment, and I was able to move forward one more step.

If you intend to be the external encouragement for a person suffering from mental health issues, it will require some sacrifice. This means that you are going to have to give up some things. This could mean time, money, or resources. It can take a lot from you and the people around you, but when you do decide to help, it can be just as rewarding for yourself as the person you are helping. When you commit to helping someone who struggles with their mental health, you also must consider your own mental health. When you are amidst the different highs and lows that your loved one experiences you need to have your own resources to fall back on. Gather people around you who can encourage you and check on you when you face challenges. Have your own network of support.

When we ask for the support, we must also sacrifice a little bit of our ego. We must stop telling ourselves the lie that we know everything or that we don't need to let others in. We must open our hearts and minds to receive help from others to get through the times when our loved one's face mountains with their mental illness. It's not easy, and I know many want to keep things close to us and not share. As I stated before, I am an introvert, so sharing is not something that comes naturally to me. When you share and ask for help, you are not giving up power. You are empowering others to help you, just as you are helping your loved ones. As I write this, a good friend of mine is relying on me to encourage him about sacrificing for his mother as she struggles with her illness. I'm proud I can be a leaning post for him as we all need people that we can lean on.

Another form of encouragement I receive is through my Faith. As a son, I love my parents. It has been hard to see my parents go through the most complex struggles with mental illness. My mother still does have her highs and lows. What's encouraging, though, is now I have help, heavenly and earthly, to aid me on this journey. Powerful encouragement can propel you towards a new victory in your life. Susan Taylor states that "seeds of faith are always within us; sometimes it takes a crisis to nourish and encourage their growth." A crisis is defined by Webster's Dictionary as "an emotionally significant event or radical change of status in a person's life."[1] When a crisis happens, it ends the usual pattern of our life. We are not conditioned to have a massive turn in our everyday life, and it makes us uncomfortable. Everyone handles a crisis differently by what they say, the way they behave, or the decisions they make. It's easy to judge someone from the outside when they are going through a crisis because everyone has different levels of tolerance or capacity. You might see someone going through something and think you could manage it better. What you would see as an opportunity, maybe losing a job or being forced to move, others might see as a major crisis. Empathy is critical during times like this as sometimes people are not looking for advice but simply need someone to be there to listen. Through my journey with my parents' mental illness, I have found my Faith, it has grown and taken a hold of my life that I could never have imagined. It was always within me, but during the tough times, I was able to encourage it to grow. Now, when I face a crisis, I know that God will be there to encourage me, along with my wife, friends, and other professionals I can lean on.

As my family struggles with mental illness, we have learned that each day will be different. There are good days and bad days, days when we encounter a crisis and days that are excellent, and days that are in between. We keep the hope alive that the stress of mental illness will not overtake the goodness in people. When we allow ourselves to hope, to be encouraged, it helps us get through the hard times. Remember to go along the journey with others to encourage you when things get complicated. This journey is not easy.

Some questions you can ask yourself after reading this chapter:

1. What is your capacity? What are the signs that let you know you have reached your limit?

2. Who can you call on for help when you are at capacity? Who can you lean on emotionally in a crisis?

3. What can you do to help you return to the baseline of your capacity?

4. Where can you find sources of encouragement and relief

CHAPTER 6: DEFINING AND OPERATING IN YOUR PURPOSE

People who struggle with mental illness have been devalued in our society for far too long. Every one of God's creations has a purpose and greatness within them. People might have struggles, and there might be times when no one wants to be around those with mental illness, but everyone was made with the potential to do wonderful things on Earth. Our tragedies and our illnesses are trying to put up roadblocks in front of us to not walk in our purpose and destiny. Many people with mental health issues can function typically today and are active in their life, career, and business. Having a mental health disease is no longer the life-ending diagnosis it was hundreds of years ago. As I mentioned before, the past treatment of those struggling with mental health illnesses has created a dark cloud over both what a diagnosis means and what treatment looks like. The more we can educate people on the current norms of treatment and what life looks like today with mental health struggles, perhaps people will be less fearful to speak their truth and seek help.

Dr. Myles Munroe states that "in order to understand

the purpose of a thing, you have to talk to the creator of the thing." He says that if you want to understand your life's purpose, you must go and talk to who created you. In my opinion, the one who created you is God Himself. When you know your purpose, how you live and conduct yourself every day becomes different. You no longer will look in the mirror and say, I do not know what I should be doing today. You will be like me, knowing that I have breath in my body what I should be doing every day. My purpose is to encourage people in their life, career, and business.

When I finished college, I decided to stay in the State of Rhode Island. To be honest with you, I became ingrained in the community. I worked, lived, was educated there, and spent most of my time in the Army National Guard. I decided to work full-time for the university that I graduated from, Johnson & Wales. Now, I was raised predominantly as a city boy in Brooklyn, NY. I was ready to earn money and be done with earning degrees. While I did grow up in a household rich in love, we were not wealthy when it came to money. I remember speaking to some of my professors after I graduated, expressing how I couldn't wait to work full time and start making some money. They stopped me in my tracks, however. They said – don't you know that a Black man with education and a master's degree can be powerful? What they were saying spoke to me, so I decided to stay in school while I worked full-time.

In 2000, I received my master's degree in Teacher Business Education. I remember most the number of family and friends that attended my graduation. They came out and held it down for me! It was a crazy year between graduating, the Y2 craze when we all thought computers would stop working, and another big life-changing event for me. That was also the year my schoolmate, Deborah, became my wife.

After I left Johnson & Wales, I sought an opportunity to work within the corporate sector. I found a job working for B.J.'s Wholesale Club, a Fortune 500 company, in their corporate office as a Senior Training Specialist. This allowed me to train managers and executives to be leaders at the company. It required a lot of travel and also flexibility because sometimes training had to be scheduled quickly. After spending some time at B.J.'s, I decided to pivot my career. I worked in the banking industry, helping small business owners find funding and providing consulting to start and grow their businesses. The banking industry was a terrific opportunity and assisted me with gaining some solid entrepreneurial skills. I loved helping small business owners and entrepreneurs realize their dreams. It was rewarding to not only do something you were educated for and have the knowledge and the experience to do, but to help others in the process. That is the reason why today, I still consult with small business owners and entrepreneurs about growing their businesses.

Understanding my purpose brought clarity and excitement. It helps guide me every day that I am walking on the Earth. Also, when you have a purpose, you have a clearer vision of your destiny. As I was thinking about my entry into Earth, I'm reminded that before God formed us in our mother's womb, He created us in the spiritual realm. He then spoke the plan he set up for our destiny. He then placed our spirit in an egg and sperm, and that thing became a living human being. We must understand that before we entered this Earth at birth, The Creator made us to do great things on Earth.

Psalm 139:13-14
"For you created my inmost being you knit me together in my mother's womb. I praise you because I am fearfully and wonderfully made; your works are wonderful; I know that well."

I think about why God decided to put me in the family in which I was born. It wasn't my choice but His. My choice lies in what I do every day and how I walk this journey with my family's struggle with mental illness. You may not understand at this point why God has given you people in your life with mental illness but trust me, there is a reason. You can choose to seek that reason and open your heart to God's purpose, or you can choose to be resistant and bitter. My family's struggles go on – I am not at the end of this journey. However, it is what we do during times of struggle that matters. When our loved ones are going through what they go through it is so easy to judge them. It's harder to listen and encourage them. I was recently having a conversation with my mother. We were discussing the struggles that my oldest brother is facing with his mental health. It is hard to see these struggles as the youngest brother. Still, I had to reflect on the good things that have happened, such as where my brother used to be in the past versus where he is now. It could be worse, and we must celebrate the small wins our loved ones make before looking for a miraculous change. Sometimes we must just take it day by day and find our peace in surviving and moving on. I used to think – woe is me I can't move past my past – but we can. Humans are designed to make mistakes and designed to grow from them. While nothing in this life is perfect, things can get better if we allow them to. I made the conscious choice to not let the past stay with me, to move forward and look for brighter things. Even while you're living the struggle every day you can still make that choice. Know that things will get better, there are people who can help you, and you can get through this.

Some questions you can ask yourself after reading this chapter are,

>1. What is your purpose in life? What do you feel called to do?

>2. What can you learn from your journey in helping friends and/or loved ones with their mental health struggles?

CHAPTER 7: IT'S NOT ABOUT HOW YOU START BUT FINISH

As we begin the closing chapter, I want to share the story of how my wife and I were blessed in an extraordinary way. We received an angel when we least expected it, in a way that I would never have predicted when I started this particular journey. This might be the getting tissues out chapter because you will see how tears of sorrow were turned into tears of joy.

When I was a deacon at my church, I was asked to join the prison ministry team. Two of my church pastors headed up the prison ministry and mobilized men to take on this challenge. They felt that I would be a good fit on the team to go into prisons and conduct Bible studies. Honestly, I did not believe I was called to be in this prison ministry. I felt that I did not have the ministry skills or the Bible insight to be in a prison ministry. I thought that I was not adequate to share with men in this environment. It just wasn't something I was passionate about, and it had never occurred to me as an aspiration, so it was hard to find excitement in the project. I did go to the ministry training and the training given by the prison personnel, and I passed. However, I still didn't feel called to do this and wasn't planning to join this ministry. But - there is always a but if you are a believer - God is never finished with his craftsmanship because he is Alpha and Omega, the beginning, and the end. God said to me - you must be obedient to your leadership; they see something in you, you can be involved in this ministry, and you are needed to do so. So, despite all my hesitation and resistance, I decided to get involved in this ministry and began teaching the Bible inside a prison.

From the first day, the experience at the prison was disconcerting. My wife dropped me off at the prison, which in itself felt very odd. It was an uncomfortable feeling to be entering a place of sorrow and fear. I didn't like going into the prison because once in, you were trapped - you had to be let out by a guard. There was no other way to leave. On one occasion we were even locked inside a room with prisoners during a Code. Even though we were trained for emergencies, it was not a good feeling, I can tell you that. During those three years of serving in the prison ministry, I never got used to going in and used to being allowed out. I was super passionate about sharing the Word of the Lord and being obedient to what the Lord was telling me to do, but I could not find my purpose in this environment. The remarkable thing about sharing with the men over those three years was the great conversations we had about hope, faith, love, and the gospels. Despite feeling like this wasn't my calling, to bring light to a place that is known for darkness was uplifting and gratifying. I can tell you that every time that I left that place, even though I never wanted to go back, I felt blessed.

Years after, I left the prison ministry. My wife and I had a good friend conducting pastoral care in the same prison system. One of her clients in the prison told her that he found out while he was incarcerated that he had a child who was taken from their mother. This man was rightly concerned about his child's future and asked our friend if she could find a good family that could adopt his daughter. My wife and I had already been licensed foster parents for almost three years and had yet to receive a child into our home who qualified for adoption. After talking about it with us, our friend passed our information to the state department handling his client's daughter's case, and we were called about fostering to adopt this child. At the time, we had a ten-year-old foster child staying with us, and we were extremely excited to provide a stable and loving home for another child. However, before we accepted, we decided we needed to get more information from the state department. My wife also did a visit to see the child, a one-year-old girl. She was lovely. We were offered to spend some time with her in our house, then an overnight stay, and then the subsequent placement in our home. We still had a minimum of six months to foster her before we could begin the process of adoption. It took us about ten months to adopt this beautiful child.

During that time, our ten-year-old foster child went back to her family, and we received our one-year-old's sister to foster. In October 2017, we adopted our Angel. We kept the name her biological mother gave her because we genuinely felt that God had given her that name. He knew she would be an angel for our family.

Many times in our lives, we do not see the vision God has for us. We take for granted the opportunities placed before us. The same place that I sowed his Word was from where we received our harvest. I mention this as encouragement. Many times, we look at the sacrifices and struggles we make for others and wonder what we will get out of it. I didn't want to minister in a prison. Every day I went there, I did not want to return. It made me uncomfortable, and I was never sure that it was what I was meant to do. I couldn't see God's plan, why he had me ministering to these men. However, I had Faith that there was a reason. That reason was one of the greatest gifts from God.

You might be looking at the struggles of someone with mental health issues and be thinking the same thing – how can I sacrifice my own comfort to help them? What will I get out of this? Is this really what I was meant to do? My advice is to have faith, accept that your sacrifices will be rewarded, and find comfort in the fact that we can be God's mercy on earth for others when we help them through their struggles. I knew I had to listen to where God was placing me. I had to put my own needs aside and sacrifice my comfort to receive my biggest blessing. Our daughter, Angel, who is six years old now, and her sister, who we also adopted, is four. My children have not only been a gift to my wife and myself but to my entire family. Ministering in the prison was an experience that ultimately changed the trajectory of my life in ways I would never have imagined. If you open yourself up to what God is asking you to do, you might find you receive joy beyond your wildest dreams.

Moving on in God's plan is not always easy. In our life, career, or business, we all experience storms now and then. If you think about the weather, all storms don't start with a high blowing wind. Some storms begin with a calm day. Then the wind starts picking up, and the clouds start picking up. Sometimes, these storms catch you off guard. You have to run for shelter, especially if you weren't planning for it. We all will go through storms in our lives. They will pop up when we least expect it. As I've said in previous chapters, being prepared for these storms of life is critical to getting past them. Using the advice I have laid out in my book, the advice I have gained from personal experience can help you be better prepared. Also, please remember, whatever you are going through, whatever your loved ones are going through, there is always sunshine after the storm. We have to be looking to the future; after the clouds have moved away, we can see the light.

As I begin to close this book, a small piece of my story, I genuinely want to thank the Lord, my family, and friends who have helped me along my journey. We often forget about the wonderful things that have come to us, such as the blessings and successes that have been impressed upon us. When life gets rough, we tend to focus on the hardest parts, not the small bits that helped us through. Without my family, I wouldn't be the man I am today. From day one, my life was going to be one filled with hardship having parents who struggled so much with mental health. I started with the odds stacked against me, but throughout my life, I have found so much to be joyful about. It's not about how we started in life or our career. It's all about the journey and how we finish.

The Kanston Family

APPENDIX A

Resources

ASHA International is an international organization that provides support to anyone suffering from mental illness. www.myasha.org

Black Emotional and Mental Health Collective is an organization intent on bringing wellness to Black and marginalized communities. Their website provides more details on resources in specific communities. **www.beam.community**. For immediate help from Black peers call the Black Line at 1-800-604-5841.

Boris Henson Foundation a pioneering Black mental health advocacy group -borislhensonfoundation.org

The Steve Fund is an organization seeking to help young at-risk people of color. www. stevefund.org/

Substance Abuse and Mental Health Services Administration The U. S. Government's organization for mental health and substance abuse support can help you find services in your area. They are open 24/hrs. a day, 7 days a week. 1-800-662-HELP (4357) or at www.samhsa.gov/find-help/national-helpline.

National Suicide Prevention Line If you or someone you know is in crisis and needs support call the crisis line at 1-800-273-TALK (8255).

Mental Health America is a non-profit organization that helps people through prevention, intervention, and access to health care resources - www.mhanational.org

APPENDIX B

Facts About Mental Health in America Today

Facts provided by The National Alliance on Mental Illness (NAMI)

- 1 in 5 adults experiences mental illness.
- 1 in 20 adults experiences serious mental illness.
- 1 in 15 adults experiences co-occurring disorders, such as mental health and addiction.
- 17% of youth ages 6-17 experience a mental health disorder.
- 17% of adults who are African American experience mental illness.
- 8.4 million people in the U.S. provide care for an adult with mental illness or emotional health issues.
- Rates of cardiovascular disease are two times higher for adults with serious mental health illness
- The pandemic has increased cases of mental health problems, particularly in youths and adolescents. More than 25% of parents say their child has seen a mental health professional during the pandemic.

APPENDIX C

Tips and Suggestions from Kareem's Experiences

- Encourage your family to be open about their mental health history. Just like physical history, mental health can be hereditary and needs to be discussed among families.

- Keep your supports and resources close at hand so that if you feel yourself escalating you can access them quickly.

- Have a plan in place in case you have a crisis. Let people who are around you daily know what to do and what to expect in a worst-case scenario. If you are caring for someone who struggles with mental health, have their plan nearby along with contacts for health care providers and other important services.

- Do not suffer in silence! Reach out to family, friends, professionals, or any of the resources provided in Appendix A.

- When you are at your capacity – stop! Do not push yourself beyond what you can manage. Take a step back, do some self-care, and be the best version of yourself so you can help others be the best versions of themselves.

APPENDIX D

GLOSSARY

Depression: feelings of severe low spirits, loss of hope and courage, extreme sadness

Manic: showing extreme energy and excitement

Bipolar Disorder: alternating periods of manic behavior and depression

Schizophrenia: a long-term mental disorder that involves a breakdown in the relation between thought, emotions, and behavior leading to misperceptions, inappropriate actions/feelings, withdrawal from reality, and personal relationships into fantasy and illusion. People suffering from schizophrenia often have delusions, hallucinations, and struggle to function in everyday life without treatment

Intergenerational cultural trauma: the idea that cultures that have suffered extreme trauma pass down the psychological effects of said trauma to future generations. Examples include those who have experienced slavery and Holocaust survivors.

Co-occurring disorders: when disorders, or diseases, happen at the same time in a person. For example, when a person struggles with both mental health illness and addictions.

APPENDIX E

WORKS CITED

Behere, Aniruddh Prakash, et al. "Effects of Family Structure on Mental Health of Children: A Preliminary Study." *Indian Journal of Psychological Medicine*, Medknow Publications & Media Pvt Ltd, 2017, https://www.ncbi.nlm.nih.gov/pmc/articles/PMC5559994/.

"Black and African American Communities and Mental Health." *Mental Health America*, Mental Health America, https://www.mhanational.org/issues/black-and-african-american-communities-and-mental-health.

Chand, Samuel R. *Leadership Pain: The Classroom for Growth*. Thomas Nelson, 2015.

"Co-Occurring: Mental Health and Substance Abuse." *Mental Health America*, Mental Health America, https://www.mhanational.org/conditions/co-occurring-mental-health-and-substance-abuse.

"Crisis, N. (2)." *Merriam-Webster* www.merriam-webster.com/dictionary/crisis.

The ESV Bible. Crossway, 2001, www.esv.org

Gavin, Kara. "A Lifeline for Primary Care amid a Crisis in Youth Mental Health." *University of Michigan Health Lab*, University of Michigan, 9 Nov. 2021, https://labblog.uofmhealth.org/rounds/a-lifeline-for-primary-care-amid-a-crisis-youth-mental-health.

Halloran, Michael J. "The Curse of Slavery Has Left an Intergenerational Legacy of Trauma and Poor Health for African Americans." *USAPP*, United States Politics and Policy, 11 Mar. 2019, https://blogs.lse.ac.uk/usappblog/2019/03/08/the-curse-of-slavery-has-left-an-intergenerational-legacy-of-trauma-and-poor-health-for-african-americans/.

Holy Bible. New International Version, Zondervan Publishing House, 1984.

Holtzman, Ellen. "A Home Way from Home." *Monitor on Psychology*, American Psychological Association, Mar. 2012, https://www.apa.org/monitor/2012/03/asylums.

Johnson, Jamie. "What Is the CLIFTONSTRENGTHS Assessment, and How Does It Work?" *Https://Www.uschamber.com/Co*, U. S Chamber of Commerce

King James Bible. Oxford University Press, 2008. (Original work published 1769)
"Let Go of The Past." *YouTube*, YouTube, 12 May 2018, https://www.youtube.com/watch?v=K5K1VSgoyzA.

Master Class. "A Guide to the 5 Levels of Maslow's Hierarchy of Needs - 2022." *Master Class*, Master Class, 8 Nov. 2020, https://www.masterclass.com/articles/a-guide-to-the-5-levels-of-maslows-hierarchy-of-needs#what-are-the-5-levels-of-maslows-hierarchy-of-needs.

Maxwell, John C. The 21 Indispensable Qualities of a Leader: Becoming the Person Others Will Want to Follow. Thomas Nelson, 2015.

"MBTI Basics." *Meyers Briggs Foundation.* 2022, https://www.myersbriggs.org/my-mbti-personality-type/mbti-basics/

"Mental Health by the Numbers." *NAMI*, National Alliance on Mental Illness, Feb. 2022, https://www.nami.org/mhstats.

Munroe, Myles. *Understanding the Purpose and Power of Men: God's Design for Male Identity.* Whitaker House, 2017.

Taylor, Susan L. *Lessons in Living.* Anchor Books, 1995.

DEDICATION

I dedicate this book to Grandpa and Grandma Kanston, Grandpa and Grandma Cody, in-laws Grandpa and Grandma Warren.

For the Cody and Kanston Family who sacrificed on many occasions to help my family get through tough times.

For Aunt Marion and Uncle Tony, and my late cousin Atiba, truly my brother, who gave up his house, space, room, and time with his parents. They and he allowed me and my brothers to stay in his home when my parents struggled with their mental illness.

I also want to thank my mother Angela for sharing details of gaps that I had during trying to remember stories as a child.

To my brothers Akbar and Hassan, thanks for rocking with me during our journey and your continuous support in my life's journeys. Love you bros.

For those who struggle or have struggled with mental illness and those families with them on the journey. This is my story of growing up with parents that have mental illness, my challenges, and triumphs.

www.ingramcontent.com/pod-product-compliance
Lightning Source LLC
LaVergne TN
LVHW051040070526
838201LV00067B/4878